Fast Recipes

50 Insanely Quick and Simple Ideas That'll Save Your Day

Eddy Morales

Table of Contents

1

ORANGE ROSEMARY PORK CHOPS

Prep and Cook Time: 25 min.

Ingredients:

- ❖ 4 (6-oz.) boneless pork chops
- ❖ 1 tablespoon chopped fresh rosemary
- ❖ 1/4 teaspoon salt
- ❖ 1/8 teaspoon ground black pepper
- ❖ 2 tablespoons olive oil
- ❖ 1 shallot, peeled and minced
- ❖ 1/3 cup beef broth
- ❖ 1/3 cup orange juice

Directions:

Season pork chops with rosemary, salt and pepper. Heat oil in a large skillet over medium-high heat.

Add chops and cook until browned and cooked through, 5 minutes per side. Remove to a serving platter and cover to keep warm.

Add shallots to the pan; sauté until shallots are soft. Add broth and orange juice, scraping to remove any browned bits from the bottom of the pan.

Boil until liquid is reduced by half, about 3 minutes. Pour over pork chops and serve garnished with extra rosemary.

2

GROUND BEEF STROGANOFF

Prep and Cook Time: 28 min.

Ingredients:

- ❖ 1 lb. ground beef

- ❖ 1/2 cup chopped onion

- ❖ 1/2 cup drained mushrooms

- ❖ 1-1/4 cups condensed Cream of Mushroom soup

- ❖ 1/4 cup water, red wine or beef broth

- ❖ 1/2 cup sour cream

Directions:

In a fry pan, brown the ground beef and onion; drain well. Stir in mushrooms, soup and water.

Cover and simmer for 15-20 minutes. Stir in sour cream; heat through, but do not boil.

Serve over noodles or rice.

3

ITALIAN CHICKEN

Prep and Cook Time: 30 min.

Ingredients:

- ❖ 4 to 6 boneless, skinless chicken breasts

- ❖ 1 lg. jar spaghetti sauce of choice

- ❖ 2 cups grated mozzarella cheese

- ❖ Parmesan cheese

- ❖ Salt, pepper, garlic

- ❖ Fettuccine noodles

Directions:

Grease large casserole dish. Season chicken breasts with salt, pepper and garlic. Place flat in casserole dish.

Bake for 20 minutes turning once.

Pour spaghetti sauce over chicken, then sprinkle generously with mozzarella cheese.

Bake until bubbly and cheese has melted. Prepare noodles according to directions and serve chicken and sauce over noodles. Top with grated parmesan cheese.

4

JAMAICAN JERKED CHICKEN

Prep and Cook Time: 28 min.

Ingredients:

- ❖ 3-1/2 pounds fresh chicken legs
- ❖ 2 tablespoons olive oil
- ❖ 2 tablespoons jerk seasoning
- ❖ 2 limes, juiced

Directions:

Preheat oven to 400°. Brush chicken with oil and sprinkle with Jerk Seasoning. Place in a shallow roasting pan and bake 30 minutes or until cooked thoroughly.

Sprinkle with lime juice and serve hot.

5

CREAMY CHICKEN & NOODLES

Prep and Cook Time: 17 min.

Ingredients:

- ❖ 1 (16 ounce) package wide egg noodles
- ❖ 2 (5 ounce) cans chunk chicken, drained
- ❖ 2 (10.75 ounce) cans condensed cream of mushroom soup
- ❖ 1/2 teaspoon garlic salt
- ❖ 1/2 teaspoon ground black pepper

Directions:

Bring a large pot of lightly salted water to a boil. Add pasta and cook for 8 to 10 minutes or until al dente; drain.

Return pasta to pot with chicken, soup, garlic salt and pepper over medium heat. Heat through, 5 minutes.

6

CREAMY RANCH SKILLET POTATOES

Prep and Cook Time: 22 min.

Ingredients:

- ❖ 4 to 5 medium potatoes, peeled and cubed
- ❖ 1/3 cup onion, chopped
- ❖ 1 envelope ranch-style dressing mix (1 ounce)
- ❖ 1/3 cup sour cream
- ❖ 2 cups milk
- ❖ 1 teaspoon parsley

Directions:

Precook potatoes in microwave or boil until slightly tender. Spray a large skillet with non-stick cooking spray.

Over medium heat, brown onions and potatoes.

Add remaining ingredients and simmer just until sauce thickens.

7

CRISPY PARMESAN FISH FILLETS

Prep and Cook Time: 28 min.

Ingredients:

- ❖ 6 (4 ounce) fine-textured fish fillets (such as flounder, sole or cod)

- ❖ 1 egg, beaten

- ❖ 1/2 cup grated Parmesan cheese

- ❖ 1/2 cup cornflake crumbs

- ❖ 1/4 teaspoon ground red pepper (optional)

Directions:

Heat oven to 450 degrees. Dip fish in egg; coat with combined cheese, crumbs and pepper. Place in greased shallow baking dish.

Bake 5 to 10 minutes or until fish flakes easily with fork.

Makes 6 servings.

Variation: Substitute the boneless skinless chicken breast halves for fish.

Decrease oven temperature to 400 degrees F. Bake 15 to 20 minutes or until chicken is cooked through.

8

EASY ENCHILADAS

Prep and Cook Time: 30 min.

Ingredients:

- ❖ 12 Corn tortillas
- ❖ 1 package enchilada sauce mix
- ❖ 1 lb. ground beef
- ❖ 2 tbl. instant minced onion or 1/2 cup chopped fresh onion
- ❖ 2 cups shredded Cheddar or Monterey Jack Cheese
- ❖ 1/4 cup chopped or sliced black olives

Directions:

In a medium, saucepan prepare enchilada sauce mix as directed on the package.

In a large fry pan, brown the ground beef and onion.

Drain excess fat. Stir 1/2 cup enchilada sauce into meat mixture. To assemble, dip each tortilla into sauce.

Spoon about 2 tbl. Meat mixture and 1 tablespoon cheese down the centre of each tortilla. Roll into thirds and place seam side down in a 9 by 13-inch baking dish.

When all tortillas are assembled, pour the remaining sauce over the top. Sprinkle with olives and extra cheese.

Cover with foil; bake for 20 minutes until heated through and the cheese is melted.

9

CHICKEN FRIED RICE

Prep and Cook Time: 22 min.

Ingredients:

- ❖ 2 teaspoons peanut oil

- ❖ 1/2 cup chopped green onions

- ❖ 1/4 cup sliced celery

- ❖ 1/4 cup chopped seeded red bell pepper

- ❖ 1 clove garlic, crushed

- ❖ 1/2 teaspoon grated gingerroot

- ❖ 1/4 teaspoon crushed red pepper flakes

- ❖ 6 tablespoons liquid egg substitute

- ❖ 3 cups cooked long-grain rice

- ❖ 2 cups diced cooked chicken

- ❖ 2 tablespoons lite soy sauce

❖ 1 teaspoon sugar

Directions:

Heat oil over medium-high heat in a large, non-stick skillet or wok. Add green onions, celery, bell pepper, garlic, ginger and red pepper flakes and sauté until tender-crisp (about 5 minutes).

Pour in egg substitute; cook, stirring occasionally, until mixture is set (about 3 minutes). Stir in rice, chicken, soy sauce and sugar; cook until heated thoroughly. Serve hot.

10

CHILI & CORNMEAL CRUSTED CHICKEN

Prep and Cook Time: 18 min.

Ingredients:

- ❖ 1-1/2 pounds fresh boneless, skinless chicken breasts, see
- ❖ cooking tip section
- ❖ 1/4 cup cornmeal
- ❖ 2 tablespoons chili powder
- ❖ 1 teaspoon cumin
- ❖ 1/8 teaspoon salt
- ❖ 1/8 teaspoon ground black pepper
- ❖ 2 eggs, beaten
- ❖ 2 tablespoons vegetable oil

Directions:

Pound chicken breasts between 2 pieces of plastic wrap or waxed paper to about ¼-inch thickness; set aside.

In a shallow dish combine cornmeal, chili powder, cumin, salt and pepper.

Dip the chicken breasts in beaten egg, then into the cornmeal mixture.

Heat oil in a large, non-stick skillet over medium-high heat.

Add chicken and cook on both sides until golden and no longer pink inside, about 10 minutes total.

11

BRUNSWICK STEW

Prep and Cook Time: 14 min.

Ingredients:

- ❖ 1 chicken (5 lbs.)
- ❖ 4 cups cold water
- ❖ 1 can condensed tomato soup
- ❖ 1 small can tomatoes
- ❖ 1 onion, sliced thin
- ❖ 1 can green lima beans
- ❖ 3 potatoes, sliced thin
- ❖ 1 tbl. sugar
- ❖ Salt & pepper
- ❖ 1 stick butter or margarine
- ❖ 1 can whole kernel corn

Directions:

Stew chicken remove from bone and cut in 1 inch pieces.

Return to kettle and add tomato soup, tomatoes, onion, lima beans, potatoes, and seasonings. Cook until vegetables are tender. Add corn and butter.

Cook 5 minutes. If desired, thicken with flour mixed with cold water. Serves 8.

12

CARIBBEAN RICE

Prep and Cook Time: 24 min.

Ingredients:

- ❖ 2 tbl. vegetable oil

- ❖ 1 tbl. julienne strips peeled fresh ginger

- ❖ 1 1/2 cups long-grain rice, rinsed well in several changes of

- ❖ water and drained

- ❖ 1 3/4 cups water

- ❖ 1/3 cup canned unsweetened coconut milk

- ❖ 1 small bay leaf

- ❖ 1/2 teaspoon salt

- ❖ Tabasco to taste

- ❖ 2 scallions, minced

- ❖ 2 tbl. minced fresh cilantro

- ❖ 1 tsp. of coconut extract (optional)

Directions:

In a medium saucepan, heat oil over moderately high heat until hot, but not smoking. Sauté ginger for about 2 minutes, stirring frequently.

Add rice and cook 2 minutes, stirring frequently.

Add water, coconut milk, bay leaf, salt, Tabasco, and extract. Bring mixture to a boil. Reduce heat to low and cook covered, 20 minutes, or until rice is tender and liquid is absorbed.

Remove pan from the heat and sprinkle rice with scallions and cilantro. Let rice stand 5 minutes and fluff with a fork. Discard bay leaf and serve.

13

ROSEMARY LAMB CHOPS

Prep and Cook Time: 15 min.

Ingredients:

- ❖ 12 lamb chops

- ❖ 6 TBS fresh lemon juice

- ❖ 3 TBS chopped fresh rosemary,

- ❖ 3 medium cloves garlic pressed, ¼ tsp salt

- ❖ ¼ tsp black pepper

Directions:

Mix together lemon juice, rosemary, pressed garlic, salt and pepper. Rub lamb chops with mixture. Set aside on plate (you might want to prepare the rest of your meal at this point).

Preheat broiler on high heat and place a metal oven-proof pan big enough to hold lamb chops under heat to get hot, about 5-7 inches from the heat source. Heat pan for about 10 minutes.

Once pan is hot, place lamb chops in pan, and return to broiler for about 4-5 minutes, depending on thickness of lamb. Lamb is cooked quickly as it is cooking on both sides at the same time. This is our (Quick Broil) cooking method.

Serves 4.

14

STIR FRIED CHICKEN & BOK CHOY

Prep and Cook Time: 20 min.

Ingredients:

- ❖ 1 cup chopped scallion

- ❖ 2 TBS fresh minced ginger

- ❖ 2 skinless, boneless chicken breasts cut into bite size

- ❖ pieces

- ❖ 1½ cups sliced fresh shiitake mushrooms

- ❖ 4 cups chopped bok choy

- ❖ 2 TBS soy sauce

- ❖ 1 TBS rice vinegar

- ❖ salt and white pepper to taste

- ❖ pinch of red pepper flakes

Directions:

Healthy Stir Fry scallion in a stainless-steel wok or sauté pan for 2 minutes and add ginger. Continue to stir fry for another minute, add chicken stirring constantly.

After about 2-3 minutes add shiitake mushrooms and bok choy. Continue to stir fry for another 3-4 minutes and add soy sauce, rice vinegar, salt and pepper. Serve.

Serves 4.

15

SOUTHWESTERN SALMON & BLACK BEANS

Prep and Cook Time: 30 min.

Ingredients:

- ❖ 1½ lb salmon cut into 4 pieces,

- ❖ skin and bones removed

- ❖ 1 small sized onion minced

- ❖ 1 small sized red bell pepper diced 1/4 inch

- ❖ 4 medium cloves garlic pressed

- ❖ ½ cup + 1 TBS chicken or vegetable broth

- ❖ 15oz can black beans, drained

- ❖ 1½ TBS red chili powder

- ❖ About 2 cups shredded romaine lettuce, outer leaves discarded

* 1 medium avocado cut into cubes

-- SAUCE --

* 2 TBS fresh cilantro chopped

* 1 TBS fresh mint chopped

* 1 TBS fresh basil chopped

* 3 TBS fresh lemon juice

* 3 TBS olive oil

* 1 TBS chopped pumpkin seeds

* salt and pepper to taste

Directions:

Season salmon with a little salt and pepper. Set aside while you chop and sauté vegetables.

Heat 1 TBS broth in a stainless steel 10–12-inch skillet.

Healthy Sauté onion, bell pepper and garlic in broth over medium heat for about 5 minutes stirring frequently.

Add ½ cup broth, drained beans, red chili powder. Cook for another 10 minutes. Season with salt and pepper to taste.

While beans are cooking preheat broiler on high. Place a metal skillet large enough for salmon under the heat to get hot. This takes about 10 minutes.

Mix in a bowl cilantro, mint, basil, lemon juice, olive oil, pumpkin seeds, salt and pepper.

Place salmon in the hot pan and return to broiler about 5 inches from the heat source for best results. This is usually the upper part of the oven or broiler. Broil salmon for about 3-4 minutes for medium doneness. This is our Quick Broil cooking method.

Serve salmon, beans and lettuce together on a plate. Top salmon and lettuce with cilantro topping.

Serves 4.

16

STIR FRIED SEAFOOD WITH ASPARAGUS

Prep and Cook Time: 25 min.

Ingredients:

- ❖ 1 medium onion cut in half and sliced medium thick

- ❖ 1 TBS chicken or vegetable broth

- ❖ 1 TBS minced fresh ginger

- ❖ 3 medium cloves garlic, chopped

- ❖ 2 cups fresh sliced shiitake mushrooms

- ❖ 1 bunch thin asparagus cut in 2" lengths (discard bottom fourth)

- ❖ ¼ cup fresh lemon juice

- ❖ 2 TBS soy sauce

- ❖ 2 TBS mirin wine

- ❖ pinch red pepper flakes

- ❖ 3/4 lb snapper fillet cut into 1 inch pieces

- ❖ 8 large scallops

- ❖ 8 large shrimp, peeled and deveined

- ❖ 1 cup cherry tomatoes cut in quarters

- ❖ ¼ cup chopped fresh cilantro

- ❖ salt and white pepper to taste

Directions:

Heat 1 TBS broth in a stainless-steel wok or 12 inch skillet. Healthy Stir Fry onion in broth over medium high heat for 2 minutes, stirring constantly. Add ginger, garlic, mushrooms and asparagus.

Continue to stir fry for another 3 minutes, stirring constantly. Add lemon juice, soy sauce, mirin, red pepper flakes, snapper, scallops, shrimp and stir to mix well.

Cover and simmer for just about 5 minutes stirring occasionally on medium heat.

Toss in tomatoes, cilantro, salt and pepper. Serve.

17

15 MINUTE ASIAN TUNA

Prep and Cook Time: 15 min.

Ingredients:

- ❖ 4 6oz tuna steaks

- ❖ 1 TBS fresh lemon juice to rub on tuna

- ❖ 1 cup minced scallion

- ❖ 3 medium cloves garlic pressed

- ❖ 1 TBS minced fresh ginger

- ❖ 2 cups thick sliced fresh shiitake mushrooms (remove stems)

- ❖ 1 TBS chicken broth

- ❖ 1 cup fresh squeezed orange juice

- ❖ 2 TBS soy sauce

- ❖ 2 TBS chopped cilantro

- ❖ salt and pepper to taste

Directions:

Rub tuna with lemon juice and season with a little salt and white pepper. Set aside.

Heat 1 TBS broth in a 10–12-inch stainless steel skillet. Healthy Sauté scallion, garlic, ginger, mushrooms in broth for about 2 minutes, stirring constantly over medium heat.

Add orange juice and cook for another 2 minutes, add rest of ingredients.

While sauce is simmering, preheat another non-stick skillet big enough to hold tuna over medium high heat for 3-4 minutes and place tuna in it. Cook for about 1½ -2 minutes and turn.

Cook for another 1½ -2 minutes. Place on plates and pour mushroom sauce over each steak. Or you can lay a bed of mushroom sauce on each plate and place tuna on top.

18

HEALTHY CAESAR SALAD

Prep and Cook Time: 10 min.

Ingredients:

- ❖ 2 large head romaine lettuce, outer leaves removed & discarded

- ❖ * (optional) 1/4 cup walnuts

-- DRESSING --

- ❖ 2 TBS roasted tahini

- ❖ 1 2oz can anchovies, drained of oil, rinsed and chopped

- ❖ 4 medium cloves garlic, chopped

- ❖ 3 TBS lemon juice

- ❖ 2 TBS balsamic vinegar

- ❖ 2 TBS extra virgin olive oil

❖ salt & cracked black pepper to taste

Directions:

Rinse lettuce, cut into bite size pieces, and dry.

Try to get lettuce as dry as possible so dressing is not diluted. If you have a salad spinner it is best.

Blend dressing ingredients together for 1-2 minutes, drizzling olive oil at end a little at a time.

Toss romaine with desired amount of dressing and walnuts if using them. There will be dressing left over.

It saves very well in your refrigerator for 2 weeks.

Serves 4.

19

BBQ MEATBALLS

Prep and Cook Time: 22 min.

Ingredients:

- ❖ 1 lb. hamburger
- ❖ 1 cup minced onion
- ❖ 1 egg
- ❖ 1/4 cup milk
- ❖ 1/4 cup bread crumbs
- ❖ 1 tsp. salt
- ❖ 1/4 tsp. pepper
- ❖ 2 tbl. cooking oil
- ❖ 2 (8 oz.) cans tomato sauce
- ❖ 1/2 cup brown sugar
- ❖ 2 tbl. vinegar

❖ 1 tsp. seasoned salt

Directions:

Combine first seven ingredients and shape into 12 meatballs.

Brown in oil in skillet, remove excess fat. Combine tomato sauce, brown sugar, vinegar and seasoned salt. Pour over meatballs.

Simmer over low heat 10-15 minutes, turning frequently until meatballs are well glazed. Serve over rice or noodles.

20

15 MINUTE TURKEY CHEF'S SALAD

Prep and Cook Time: 15 min.

Ingredients:

- ❖ ½ lb mixed salad greens

- ❖ 1 cup fresh basil leaves torn into pieces

- ❖ ¾ lb sliced turkey breast

- ❖ 1 small jar of prepared roasted peppers, (about 7 oz)

- ❖ 4 oz Kalamata olives

- ❖ ½ basket cherry tomatoes, cut in half

- ❖ 1 medium avocado cut into cubes

- ❖ *optional 4 oz goat cheese

- ❖ 2 TBS balsamic vinegar

- ❖ 2 TBS extra virgin olive oil

- ❖ Salt and cracked black pepper to taste

Directions:

Rinse and dry salad greens. This is done best in a salad spinner.

Divide between 4 plates, top with rest of ingredients. Whisk together vinegar, oil, salt and pepper and drizzle on top of salad.

Serves 4.

21

POACHED EGGS, COLLARD GREENS & SHIITAKE MUSHROOMS

Prep and Cook Time: 20 min.

Ingredients:

- ❖ 6 cups chopped collard greens (stems removed)

- ❖ 1 medium onion cut in half and sliced thin

- ❖ 6 fresh shiitake mushrooms, sliced medium thick stems removed

- ❖ 4 fresh free range chicken eggs

- ❖ about 4 cups water

- ❖ 1 TBS apple cider vinegar, or any white wine vinegar

-- DRESSING --

- ❖ 1 TBS fresh lemon juice

- ❖ 1 TBS minced fresh ginger

- ❖ 3 medium cloves garlic pressed

- ❖ 1 TBS soy sauce

- ❖ 1 TBS extra virgin olive oil

- ❖ salt and white pepper to taste

Directions:

Bring lightly salted water to a boil in a steamer. Rinse greens well, fold leaves in half and pull or cut out stem. Discard stems.

Chop leaf and steam for about 7 minutes. Add mushrooms, onion and steam for another 5 minutes.

While steaming greens, get ready for poaching by bringing water and vinegar to a fast simmer in a small, shallow pan.

You can start on high heat, and once it comes to a boil, reduce heat to a simmer before adding eggs. Make sure there is enough water to cover eggs.

Mix lemon juice, ginger, garlic, soy sauce, olive oil, salt, and pepper in a small bowl.

When greens are almost done poach eggs until desired doneness. This will take about 5 minutes, or just until the white is set, and the yolk has filmed over.

Press greens with back of a spoon slightly to remove excess water.

Remove vegetables from steamer, then toss with dressing. Remove eggs from water with a slotted spoon and place on plate of tossed greens.

Serves 4.

22

ITALIAN TOFU FRITTATA

Prep and Cook Time: 30 min.

Ingredients:

- ❖ 1 cup onion, chopped fine
- ❖ 4 cloves garlic, minced
- ❖ 1 cup zucchini, diced
- ❖ 1 cup red bell pepper, diced
- ❖ 2 cups finely chopped kale, (remove stems)
- ❖ 1 cup chopped fresh tomato
- ❖ ¼ cup chicken or vegetable broth
- ❖ 2 TBS red wine vinegar
- ❖ 5 oz firm light tofu, drained
- ❖ 4 egg whites
- ❖ 1 TBS dried Italian seasoning

- ❖ ¼ tsp turmeric

- ❖ salt and white pepper to taste

- ❖ 2 TBS chopped fresh parsley

Directions:

Prepare vegetables by chopping them and having them ready.

Puree tofu with egg whites, Italian seasoning and turmeric in blender.

In 10-inch stainless steel pan, Healthy Sauté onion, garlic, zucchini, bell pepper, kale, and tomato for about 1 minute over medium low heat, stirring often.

Add broth and red wine vinegar. Pour tofu mixture over vegetables, cover and cook over low heat until mixture is completely firm and cooked, about 12 minutes. Top with chopped parsley.

Serves 4.

23

BREAKFAST BAGEL

Prep and Cook Time: 15 min.

Ingredients:

- ❖ 2 whole wheat bagels

- ❖ 4 large free-range chicken eggs

- ❖ 1 tsp apple cider vinegar, or any light vinegar

- ❖ 1 large tomato, sliced

- ❖ 1 bunch arugula

- ❖ 2 TBS extra virgin olive oil

- ❖ 2 medium cloves garlic, pressed

- ❖ salt and black pepper to taste

Directions:

Bring water and 1 tsp vinegar to a light boil in a shallow pan. Make sure there is enough water to cover eggs.

While water is coming to a boil, slice bagels in half and toast. Press garlic into oil and brush on cut side of toasted bagels.

Garnish bagel with arugula and sliced tomato.

To poach eggs, crack into water and cook about 5 minutes, just until the white is set, and the yolk has filmed over.

Remove with slotted spoon. Place on top of bagel and vegetables. Season with salt and pepper to taste. Serve open faced.

Serves 4.

24

ANGEL HAIR PASTA WITH LEMON CHICKEN

Prep and Cook Time: 20 min.

Ingredients:

- ❖ 1 pkg. (9 oz.) refrigerated Angel Hair Pasta

- ❖ 1-1/2 cups cooked diced chicken

- ❖ 1/3 cup butter, melted

- ❖ 2 tablespoons lemon juice

- ❖ 2 tablespoons chopped fresh parsley, (or 1 teaspoon dried

- ❖ parsley)

- ❖ 1/4 teaspoon marjoram

- ❖ 1/4 teaspoon garlic powder

Directions:

Prepare pasta according to package directions.

Toss pasta with remaining ingredients. Season with salt and ground black pepper.

25

BASIL FRITTATA

Prep and Cook Time: 15 min.

Ingredients:

- ❖ ½ medium onion, minced

- ❖ 1+1 TBS chicken broth

- ❖ 3 medium cloves garlic, pressed

- ❖ 1 cup thinly sliced crimini mushrooms

- ❖ ½ medium tomato, seeds removed, and diced

- ❖ 3 large eggs

- ❖ 3 TBS chopped fresh basil

- ❖ salt and black pepper to taste

Directions:

Heat 1 TBS broth in a 10-inch stainless steel skillet.

Healthy Sauté onion over medium how heat 3 minutes, stirring frequently. Add garlic, mushrooms and continue to sauté for another 2 minutes.

Add 1 TBS broth, tomato, salt, pepper and cook for another minute. Stir well, and gently scrape pan with a wooden spoon to remove any slight burning.

Beat eggs well, and season with salt and pepper. Mix in chopped basil. Pour eggs over vegetables evenly and turn heat to low. Cover and cook for about 5 minutes, or until firm. Cut into wedges and serve.

Serves 2.

26

BAKED PASTA IN A HURRY

Prep and Cook Time: 30 min.

Ingredients:

- ❖ 1 Large jar chunky or thick spaghetti sauce

- ❖ 1- 1/2 cups water

- ❖ 1 bag pasta (shells, bow-tie, etc.)

- ❖ 2 cups shredded Mozzarella cheese

- ❖ Parmesan cheese

Directions:

Lightly coat large baking dish with Crisco to make clean up easy. Heat oven to 425.

In a mixing bowl, stir sauce, water and pasta until well coated. Pour pasta & sauce into a baking dish.

Cover with foil and bake for 30 minutes. Top with shredded cheese, return to oven for 10 minutes.

Sprinkle with Parmesan and serve.

27

15 MINUTE BROILED CHICKEN SALAD

Prep and Cook Time: 15 min.

Ingredients:

- ❖ 4 boneless chicken breasts
- ❖ ½ lb mixed salad greens
- ❖ ¼ cup sliced fresh basil leaves
- ❖ 2 TBS fresh oregano leaves
- ❖ 2 oz gorgonzola cheese
- ❖ 2 TBS fresh lemon juice
- ❖ salt and cracked black pepper to taste

-- DRESSING --

- ❖ 2 TBS fresh lemon juice
- ❖ 1 TBS extra virgin olive oil

❖ salt and cracked black pepper to taste

Directions:

Preheat broiler on high with rack in the middle of the oven, about 7 inches from heat source. Place shallow metal ovenproof pan under the heat to get very hot for about 10 minutes.

While pan is getting hot, rinse and spin dry salad greens along with basil and oregano leaves. For oregano, simply run your fingers down the stem to remove leaves and place whole in salad.

When pan is hot, reduce heat to low, season chicken breasts with a little salt and pepper and place on hot pan skin side up. Return to broiler and cook for 15 minutes, or until done, depending on the thickness of the breasts.

The breasts cook fast because they are cooking on both sides at the same time. This is our Quick Broil cooking method. When chicken is just about done, remove skin and top breasts with a little gorgonzola cheese and return to broiler to melt. (If you are not sure if chicken is done, make a little slice with a small sharp knife to check. It should be only slightly pink.

Toss greens with lemon juice, olive oil, salt and pepper. Distribute greens onto 4 plates.

Place chicken breasts on top of greens. Serve.

Serves 4.

28

BEEF & VEGETABLE STIR FRY

Prep and Cook Time: 23 min.

Ingredients:

- ❖ 1 beef bouillon cube
- ❖ 1/4 cup hot water
- ❖ 3 tablespoons reduced-sodium soy sauce
- ❖ 2 tablespoons dry white wine or water
- ❖ 1 tablespoon cornstarch
- ❖ 1/4 to 1/2 teaspoon ground ginger
- ❖ 1/4 teaspoon ground black pepper
- ❖ 1/4 tablespoon vegetable oil
- ❖ 1 pound lean beef sirloin steak, cut into 2-inch strips
- ❖ 2 cloves garlic, finely chopped
- ❖ 2 tablespoons water

- ❖ 1 package (16 oz.) frozen mixed vegetables

- ❖ 1/2 cup (about 3) 1-inch slices green onions

- ❖ 4 cups cooked brown rice

Directions:

Dissolve bouillon in 1/4 cup water in a small bowl. Stir in soy sauce, wine, corn-starch, ginger, and pepper.

Heat vegetable oil in a large, non-stick skillet over medium high heat. Add beef and garlic; cook, stirring constantly, for 3 to 4 minutes or until beef is no longer pink. Remove from skillet.

Heat 2 tablespoons water in same skillet. Add vegetables; cook, stirring occasionally, for 3 to 5 minutes or until vegetables are tender.

Return beef to skillet; stir in bouillon mixture and green onions. Cook, stirring frequently, for 2 to 3 minutes or until sauce is thickened. Serve over rice.

29

GOLDEN SQUASH SOUP

Prep and Cook Time: 30 min.

Ingredients:

- ❖ 1 medium sized butternut squash, peeled and cut into about ½
- ❖ inch pieces (about 3 cups)
- ❖ 1 large onion, chopped
- ❖ 3 medium cloves garlic, chopped
- ❖ 1 TBS chopped fresh ginger
- ❖ 1 tsp turmeric
- ❖ 1 tsp curry powder
- ❖ 2 3/4 cups + 1 TBS chicken or vegetable broth
- ❖ 6 oz canned coconut milk
- ❖ 2 TBS chopped fresh cilantro

- ❖ salt & white pepper to taste

Directions:

Peel squash and cut into pieces.

Heat 1 TBS broth in medium soup pot. Healthy Sauté onion in broth over medium heat for 5 minutes, stirring frequently, until translucent.

Add garlic, ginger, and continue to sauté for another minute. Add turmeric, curry powder, and mix well. Add squash and broth, and mix. Bring to a boil on high heat.

Once it comes to a boil reduce heat to medium low and simmer uncovered until squash is tender, about 10 minutes.

Place in blender and blend with coconut milk. Make sure you blend in batches filling blender only half full.

Start on low speed, so hot soup does not erupt and burn you. Blend until smooth, about 1 minute.

Thin with a little broth if needed. Season to taste with salt and white pepper. Reheat, and add cilantro.

Serves 4-6

30

ZESTY MEXICAN SOUP

Prep and Cook Time: 28 min.

Ingredients:

- ❖ 1 medium onion minced

- ❖ 4 medium cloves garlic, chopped

- ❖ 2 TBS red chili powder

- ❖ 3 cups + 1 TBS chicken, or vegetable broth

- ❖ 1 small to medium green bell pepper diced, 1/4 inch pieces

- ❖ 1 small zucchini diced, 1/4 inch pieces

- ❖ 1 cup finely chopped collard greens

- ❖ 1 15oz can diced tomatoes

- ❖ 1 15oz can rinsed black beans

- ❖ 1 cup frozen yellow corn

- ❖ 1 4oz can diced green chili

- ❖ 1 tsp dried oregano, 1 tsp cumin

- ❖ 1/4 cup chopped pumpkin seeds

- ❖ 1/2 cup chopped fresh cilantro

- ❖ salt and pepper to taste

Directions:

Heat 1 TBS broth in a medium soup pot.

Healthy Sauté onion, garlic, and green peppers in broth over medium heat for 5 minutes, stirring often.

Add red chili powder, mix in well and add broth, zucchini, collard greens and tomatoes.

Cook for another 5 minutes and add beans, corn, green chili, oregano, and cumin.

Bring to a boil on high heat. Once it begins to boil, reduce heat to medium low and simmer uncovered for 15 minutes longer (Simmering uncovered enhances flavour).

Add chopped cilantro, pumpkin seeds, salt and pepper. Serves 6.

31

BAKED HALIBUT WITH HERBS

Prep and Cook Time: 30 min.

Ingredients:

- ❖ 1 1/2 lbs halibut steak or fillet, cut into 8 pieces
- ❖ ¼ cup chicken or vegetable stock
- ❖ 2 TBS lemon juice
- ❖ 3 medium cloves garlic, pressed
- ❖ 2 TBS capers
- ❖ 2 TBS chopped fresh parsley
- ❖ 1 TBS chopped fresh tarragon
- ❖ 1 TBS chopped fresh chives
- ❖ salt and pepper to taste

Directions:

Preheat oven to 450. Place the fish in a baking dish just large enough to hold them, add the remaining ingredients.

Cover, and bake until done, about 15 minutes; do not overcook. Serve at once, pouring the pan juices over the fish.

Serves 4.

32

BAKED CHICKEN BREAST WITH HONEY MUSTARD SAUCE

Prep and Cook Time: 30 min.

Ingredients:

- ❖ 4 boneless, skinless chicken breasts
- ❖ 1 ½ cups chicken broth
- ❖ 1 TBS fresh lemon juice
- ❖ 2 ½ TBS honey
- ❖ 2 TBS Dijon mustard
- ❖ ¼ cup sliced dried apricots
- ❖ 2 TBS coarsely chopped walnuts
- ❖ 1 TBS chopped parsley
- ❖ 4 bunches fresh spinach, stems removed and rinsed thoroughly

- ❖ salt and pepper to taste

Directions:

Preheat oven to 375. Place chicken breasts in baking dish.

Season with salt and pepper and cover. Bake for about 30 minutes, or until done. While chicken is baking, bring salted water to a boil to cook spinach.

While water is coming to a boil, begin sauce. Combine broth, lemon juice, honey, and mustard in a small saucepan.

Whisk together and bring to a boil on high heat. Once it comes to a boil, simmer for about 20 minutes. This can be cooking while chicken is baking.

You want it to be reduced to a little less than half the volume you start with. This will thicken and intensify the flavour.

Add apricots and cook on high for another 5 minutes. When sauce is done add chopped walnuts, parsley, salt and pepper.

Cook spinach for only 2 minutes at the most. Drain and press dry. Season with a little salt and pepper.

Divide spinach between 4 plates. Slice chicken breast and place over bed of spinach. Spoon sauce over chicken and spinach.

Serves 4.

33

BEEF STEW IN A HURRY

Prep and Cook Time: 27 min.

Ingredients:

- ❖ 1 can (1 lb.) sliced carrots

- ❖ 1 can (8 oz.) whole potatoes

- ❖ 1 can (8 oz.) cut green beans

- ❖ 1/4 cup all-purpose flour

- ❖ 1 envelope dry onion soup mix

- ❖ 3 cups cut-up cooked beef

Directions:

Drain vegetables, reserving liquid. Combine flour and soup mix in large skillet.

Add water to reserved liquid to measure 3 cups; stir into mixture in skillet.

Heat to boiling, stirring constantly. Boil and stir 1 minute. Stir in vegetables and beef.

Cover; cook over low heat about 10 minutes or until it is heated through. 4 servings, about 1-1/2 cups each.

34

BLUE RIBBON CHILI

Prep and Cook Time: 30 min.

Ingredients:

- ❖ 2 pounds ground beef

- ❖ 1/2 onion, chopped

- ❖ 1 teaspoon ground black pepper

- ❖ 1/2 teaspoon garlic salt

- ❖ 2 1/2 cups tomato sauce

- ❖ 1 (8 ounce) jar salsa

- ❖ 4 tablespoons chili seasoning mix

- ❖ 1 (15 ounce) can light red kidney beans

- ❖ 1 (15 ounce) can dark red kidney beans

Directions:

In a large saucepan over medium heat, combine the ground beef and the onion and sauté for 10 minutes, or until meat is browned and onion is tender. Drain grease, if desired.

Add the ground black pepper, garlic salt, tomato sauce, salsa, chili seasoning mix and kidney beans.

Mix well, reduce heat to low and simmer for 20 minutes.

35

BREAKFAST BURRITOS

Prep and Cook Time: 17 min.

Ingredients:

- ❖ 4 slices turkey bacon
- ❖ 2 flour tortillas (7 inch)
- ❖ 2 Tbl. shredded Sharp Cheddar Cheese
- ❖ 1 large egg white
- ❖ 1 Tbl. chopped green chilies

Directions:

Cook turkey bacon in a non-stick skillet on medium heat 8 to 10 minutes or until lightly browned. Place 2 turkey bacon slices on each tortilla; sprinkle with cheese.

Beat egg and chilies; add to hot skillet.

Cook and stir 2 minutes or until set. Divide egg mixture between tortillas; fold tortillas over filling.

Top with Salsa, if desired.

36

CHEESE & CORN QUESADILLAS

Prep and Cook Time: 19 min.

Ingredients:

- ❖ 4 (10-in.) flour tortillas
- ❖ 1 can (15-oz.) corn, drained
- ❖ 1-1/2 cups shredded Monterey Jack cheese
- ❖ 2 medium roma tomatoes, seeded and diced

Directions:

Preheat oven to 350°F. Spray 2 baking sheets with vegetable cooking spray.

Place tortillas on prepared baking sheets. Evenly sprinkle each tortilla with corn, cheese and tomatoes.

Bake for 4 minutes, or until cheese begins to melt and tortilla is still pliable. Fold tortilla in half.

Carefully flip tortilla over and bake another 5 minutes. Cut each quesadilla into 4 wedges; serve warm.

37

CHICKEN BURRITOS

Prep and Cook Time: 18 min.

Ingredients:

- ❖ 1 tablespoon vegetable oil
- ❖ 1 pound boneless, skinless chicken breast halves, cut into 2- inch strips
- ❖ 1-1/4 cups water
- ❖ 1 package (1.5-oz.) Taco Seasoning Mix
- ❖ 8 (10-in.) burrito-size flour tortillas, warmed

Directions:

Heat vegetable oil in large skillet over medium-high heat. Add chicken; cook for 3 to 4 minutes or until no longer pink.

Add water and seasoning mix. Bring to a boil.

Reduce heat to low; cook for 3 to 4 minutes or until mixture thickens.

Spoon chicken mixture evenly over tortillas. Top with shredded cheddar cheese, shredded lettuce, chopped green onions, sliced olives and Salsa, if desired. Fold into burritos.

38

CHICKEN CURRY IN A HURRY

Prep and Cook Time: 25 min.

Ingredients:

- ❖ 2 teaspoons brown sugar

- ❖ 2 teaspoons curry powder

- ❖ 1/2 teaspoon dry mustard

- ❖ 1/4 teaspoon pepper

- ❖ 4 boneless chicken breast halves, cut in bite-size pieces

- ❖ 14.5 ounces chicken broth or about 1-3/4 cups

- ❖ 1 1/2 cups orange juice

- ❖ 1 1/4 cups long grained rice, uncooked

- ❖ 10 ounce package frozen Peas

Directions:

Combine first 5 ingredients; sprinkle 1 tbsp seasoning mixture over chicken, tossing to coat. Reserve remaining seasoning mixture.

Bring chicken broth, orange juice, rice and reserved seasoning mixture to a boil in a large non-stick skillet.

Add chicken; reduce heat, cover simmer 15 minutes.

Stir in peas; cover and simmer 10 minutes or until liquid is absorbed.

39

COCONUT SHRIMP

Prep and Cook Time: 30 min.

Ingredients:

- ❖ 40 medium shrimp
- ❖ 2 tsp. garlic and herb seasoning
- ❖ 1 tsp. black pepper
- ❖ 1-1/2 cups flour
- ❖ 4 medium eggs, well-beaten
- ❖ 2 cups shredded coconut

Directions:

Preheat oven to 400°F. Spray a large baking sheet with non-stick spray. Sprinkle garlic and herb seasoning and pepper evenly over the shrimp.

Place flour, egg, and coconut in three small separate bowls. Dip shrimp into the egg, then the flour, then the egg again, and then into the coconut.

Place shrimp on baking sheet at least 1 inch apart. Bake for about 12-15 minutes, or until they are crisp and golden brown.

Serving suggestion: dip in mango sauce.

40

CORNMEAL WAFFLES

Prep and Cook Time: 20 min.

Ingredients:

- ❖ 1 cup yellow cornmeal

- ❖ 1 cup flour

- ❖ 2 tablespoons sugar

- ❖ 4 teaspoons baking powder

- ❖ 1/2 teaspoon salt

- ❖ 1-3/4 cups milk

- ❖ 2 eggs, lightly beaten

- ❖ 1/3 cup butter, melted

Directions:

In a large bowl, combine cornmeal, flour, sugar, baking powder and salt.

In a separate bowl with an electric mixer at medium speed, beat together milk, eggs and butter.

Add to dry ingredients and mix to blend. Pour batter onto a hot, greased waffle iron and bake until browned and crisp. Serve with butter and syrup or jam.

41

GARLIC MASHED POTATOES

Prep and Cook Time: 25 min.

Ingredients:

- ❖ 2 pounds potatoes, peeled and cut into large chunks
- ❖ 8 cloves garlic, peeled and smashed
- ❖ 1/4 cup whipping cream
- ❖ 2 tablespoons butter, softened
- ❖ 1/2 teaspoon salt
- ❖ 1/4 teaspoon ground black pepper

Directions:

Add potatoes and garlic to a large saucepan; cover with 2 inches of water.

Bring to a boil and simmer until tender, about 15 to 20 minutes.

Drain well and put back in pan. Add milk, butter, salt and pepper; mash with a potato masher until creamy. Serve immediately.

42

GLAZED MICROWAVE CHICKEN

Prep and Cook Time: 20 min.

Ingredients:

- ❖ 4 boneless and skinless chicken breasts
- ❖ 2 tsp. paprika
- ❖ 8 thin lemon slices
- ❖ 1/4 cup honey
- ❖ 1/4 cup spicy brown mustard
- ❖ 1/4 tsp. onion powder
- ❖ 1 tsp. lemon juice
- ❖ 1 tsp. curry powder

Directions:

Sprinkle chicken breasts with paprika and then top with lemon slices.

Place in microwave dish, cover loosely with wax paper, and microwave for about 8-10 minutes, turning dish halfway through cooking.

Remove chicken from the dish; (leave behind any liquid).

In a small microwave bowl, mix remaining ingredients.

Microwave the sauce for 2 minutes. Spoon sauce over chicken and microwave again for about 2 minutes, or until the glaze is hot and a fork can be inserted into the chicken with ease.

43

MANDARIN PORK CHOPS

Prep and Cook Time: 29 min.

Ingredients:

- ❖ 4 pork chops

- ❖ 1 tablespoon oil

- ❖ 1/2 cup orange juice

- ❖ 1/4 cup water

- ❖ 3 tablespoons brown sugar

- ❖ 2 tablespoons lemon juice

- ❖ 1 tablespoon cornstarch

- ❖ 2 chicken bouillon cubes, crushed

- ❖ 11 fluid ounces Mandarin orange sections

- ❖ 1 green bell pepper, sliced

Directions:

In a large skillet, brown pork chops in oil; remove from the pan.

Add orange juice, water, brown sugar, lemon juice, corn-starch, and crushed chicken bouillon cubes to the skillet. Cook and stir until slightly thickened.

Return the pork chops, cover, and simmer for 20 minutes, or until tender.

Add mandarin orange sections (drained) and sliced green bell pepper; heat through.

44

MEATBALLS AND RICE

Prep and Cook Time: 24 min.

Ingredients:

- ❖ 1 package hamburger
- ❖ 1 package beefy onion soup mix
- ❖ 2 cans cream of mushroom soup
- ❖ 1 cup rice

Directions:

Mix hamburger and soup mix. Roll meat into ½" balls. Brown in pan, until fully cooked. Add cream of mushroom soup.

Cook until soup is bubbly. Cook rice according to package directions.

Serve meatballs and gravy over rice. Add your favourite vegetable on the side and you have got a great meal!

45

MEXICAN CHICKEN PIZZA

Prep and Cook Time: 20 min.

Ingredients:

- ❖ 1 package taco seasoning (DO NOT use if using pre-seasoned chicken)
- ❖ 1-1/2 cups Thick-n-Chunky style salsa
- ❖ 1 can refrigerated pizza crust
- ❖ 1 cup grated Monterey Jack cheese
- ❖ 1 cup grated Velveeta cheese

Directions:

Preheat oven to 425 degrees. Unroll dough, place on pizza or baking pan, pressing dough until thin crust is formed to edge of pan.

Bake crust for 8 minutes or until crust begins to brown.

Brown chicken; mix in taco seasoning. Spread salsa on crust, followed by chicken and cheeses.

Return to oven, bake additional 7-12 minutes, or until edges of crust are golden brown and cheese is melted.

46

WHIPPED SWEET POTATO CASSEROLE

Prep and Cook Time: 30 min.

Ingredients:

- ❖ 2 pounds sweet potatoes, peeled and cubed

- ❖ 2 tablespoons orange juice

- ❖ 3/4 cup brown sugar

- ❖ 1/8 teaspoon ground nutmeg

- ❖ 2 tablespoons butter, cubed

- ❖ 1 cup miniature marshmallows

Directions:

Preheat oven to 350 degrees F (175 degrees C).

In a large saucepan cook sweet potatoes in salted water over medium high heat for about 20 minutes, or until done.

Drain, and add orange juice, brown sugar, nutmeg and butter. Whip until smooth.

Spread into a medium size casserole dish and top with marshmallows.

Bake in preheated oven for about 10 minutes, or until marshmallows are golden brown.

47

TUNA TORTELLINI SALAD

Prep and Cook Time: 25 min.

Ingredients:

- ❖ 1 pkg.(20 oz.) refrigerated family size Three Cheese

- ❖ Tortellini, cooked, rinsed and drained

- ❖ 1/2 pound green beans, cut into 1-inch pieces, cooked

- ❖ 2 cans (6 1/8 oz. each) solid white tuna packed in water, drained

- ❖ 1 large chopped tomato, diced

- ❖ 3/4 cup sliced ripe black olives, sliced

- ❖ 4 green onions, sliced

- ❖ 3/4 cup mayonnaise

- ❖ 3 tablespoons balsamic vinegar

- ❖ 3/4 teaspoon celery salt

- ❖ 1 small can corn

Directions:

Combine tortellini, green beans, tuna, tomato, olives corn and onion in a large bowl.

Combine mayonnaise, vinegar and celery salt in a small bowl.

Stir mayonnaise mixture into pasta mixture. Season with salt and pepper.

48

TUNA & TARRAGON SALAD SANDWICHES

Prep and Cook Time: 18 min.

Ingredients:

- ❖ 1 can 6-oz. tuna, drained
- ❖ 1 small tomato, chopped
- ❖ 2 tablespoons chopped trimmed green onions
- ❖ 2 tablespoons mayonnaise
- ❖ 1/4 teaspoon crushed dried tarragon
- ❖ 1/8 teaspoon salt
- ❖ 1/8 teaspoon ground black pepper
- ❖ 4 slices French bread

Directions:

Combine all ingredients in a large mixing bowl except bread; mix well.

Spread mixture on bread and serve.

49

SPEEDY CHILI

Prep and Cook Time: 24 Min.

Ingredients:

- ❖ 1 lb. ground beef
- ❖ 2 tbl. instant minced onion or 1/2 cup onion, chopped
- ❖ 1/2 cup celery
- ❖ 2 cups 1-1/4 cups tomato soup (10 3/4 oz. can)
- ❖ 2 cups (15 oz. can) kidney beans
- ❖ 2 tsp. chili powder
- ❖ 1 tsp. salt
- ❖ dash pepper

Directions:

In a large fry pan, brown ground beef, onion and celery. Drain excess fat.

Add remaining ingredients and mix well.

Cover and simmer 15 to 20 minutes to heat well.

50

EASY PANCAKES

Ingredients:

- ❖ WHEAT flour
- ❖ Water
- ❖ Fresh pasteurized EGGS,
- ❖ Skimmed MILK powder
- ❖ Clarified BUTTER
- ❖ Salt, Palm oil, Sugar

Directions:

Grease a non-stick pan and heat it over medium-low heat. Cut a corner of the bag, fill a coffee cup up to 3/4 full and pour the contents into the centre of hot pan.

Cook for about a minute and when the first bubbles appear and the dough in contact with the pan is golden, turn the pancake with the help of a spatula and cook for another minute until golden brown.

Lightning Source UK Ltd.
Milton Keynes UK
UKHW021854010321
379622UK00004B/659